I0503451

Fix Your Network Marketing Business

*Fire Up Your Team, Increase Recruiting
and Sales, and Get Your Business
Growing Again—Even if Nobody is
Doing Anything*

David M. Ward

ISBN-13: 978-1545410622
ISBN-10: 1545410623

Free Recruiting Tips Newsletter
http://recruitandgrowrich.com/newsletter

Fix Your Network Marketing Business

Golden Lantern Books
www.goldenlanternbooks.com
www.recruitandgrowrich.com

Contents

How I fixed my network marketing business

I remember it like it was yesterday. I was at a company event where I was again recognized as a top recruiter for the month. Everyone was congratulating me, asking how I did it, telling me they wish they could do what I was doing.

"If they only knew what was really going on," I thought.

Yes, I was signing up a lot of distributors. Unfortunately, nobody was doing anything.

My back office was filled with a bunch of zeros. My "team" wasn't recruiting or selling. They weren't coming to events or getting on team calls. Nobody was putting me on the phone with prospects.

My business was broken and I didn't know what to do.

Everyone I signed up had told me they wanted the same things I wanted. They wanted passive income so they didn't have to work all the time. They wanted residual income for retirement. They wanted a business that allowed them to work part time and that didn't interfere with their current job or business.

When I showed them the business opportunity, they liked what they saw and signed up.

So why weren't they doing anything?

I was confused and frustrated. I had to be doing something wrong. Maybe I was recruiting people who weren't "hungry " enough. Maybe I wasn't training them properly. Maybe I wasn't staying in touch with them enough.

I thought about quitting. But I didn't want to quit, I wanted to figure out what was wrong and fix it.

After the event, as I was leaving the hotel, I saw one of the company leaders walking towards the exit. Ron had a sales background and a lot of network marketing experience. He had been successful in our business right from the start, earning six-figures his first year. I asked if I could speak with him for a few minutes. We sat down and I told him my story.

I explained that in my first six months I had recruited 50 distributors, most of whom were smart and influential people with big lists. I told him I was making money but my business wasn't growing because I was the only one doing anything.

Ron listened and asked questions. Then he told me the facts of life about network marketing.

He said I was doing the most important thing right (recruiting) but there were a few things I needed to change about what I was doing. And then he told me things I'd never heard before.

I "got it". What he said made so much sense. In fact, I remember thinking, "Why didn't someone tell me this when I was getting started?"

When he was done, I felt a lot better. I was relieved and excited. I knew that I could get my team recruiting and selling and I knew how to do it.

I had a plan.

I followed the plan and within a few weeks, things started happening. My team actually put some sales on the books. They started recruiting, too.

Over the next few months my team continued to grow and so did my income. In my first six months in the business, most of my income came from my own effort. Now, most of my income was coming from my team.

I kept going (and kept recruiting) and within a few years, I was earning a six-figure passive income.

In this book, I'm going to tell you what Ron told me. I'll also share some insights and lessons I've learned from building my business and working with my team.

You can fix your business

You probably picked up this book because your business needs some help. Does any of this sound familiar?

— You've got distributors who sign up and do nothing
— Nobody is ordering product or tools, or they order them and don't use them
— Your team isn't coming to meetings or getting on conference calls
— You're the only one who is consistently working the business
— You've got distributors who won't return your calls
— You're sick and tired of the excuses people make for not showing up

— You're doing the work but not making any money (or you're making some money but your team isn't growing)

If any of this describes your network marketing business, this is the book for you.

You can fix your business, like I fixed mine.

If you're frustrated right now, I want you to know that you are closer to success than you realize. You know how to recruit. You know how to make money. You know what works, and what doesn't.

You may be disappointed with your results, but everything you've learned and everything you've done so far has prepared you for success.

You haven't failed. The only ones who fail are the ones who quit. The fact that you're reading this book proves that you don't want to quit, you want to figure things out.

You can do that. I'll show you how.

Who am I?

I started my professional career as an attorney. After more than twenty years in private practice, I was successful but burned out. I was fed up with the long hours and constant stress and I started looking for a plan b.

Network marketing offered me exactly what I was looking for. Once I figured out how this business really works, I was able to build a successful business that allowed me to retire from the practice of law. Today, I spend most of my time writing.

I've written other books on network marketing. They show you how I recruited and built my business. After you finish this book, please take a look:

Recruit and Grow Rich: How to Quickly Build a Successful Network Marketing Business by Recruiting Smarter, Not Working Harder

http://recruitandgrowrich.com/kindle

Recruiting Up: How I Recruited Hundreds of Professionals in my Network Marketing Business, and How You Can, Too

http://recruitingup.com

Network Marketing Made Simple: A Guide for Training New Distributors

http://recruitandgrowrich.com/nmms

Slowing down to speed up

Have you ever heard the expression, "Slowing down to speed up?" It means standing down from your regular activities and investing a few hours or a day or two examining what you're doing and planning your next steps.

That's what you're doing right now.

You're reading this book. You may go over your notes from trainings. You may talk to one or more leaders in your company. You may take an honest look at your numbers and get clear about what you need to change.

By taking time to do these things, when you get back to work, you'll have clarity about what's important and what's not important, so you can focus on things that really work. In doing that, you'll also eliminate things that waste time and cause you stress. As a result, you'll be able to get more results in less time. You slow down so you can speed up.

When I finished my meeting with Ron, I wrote down what we had talked about and made a list of things I needed to do. I stopped second guessing myself or worrying about the past. I had a plan and I got to work.

My goal with this book is to help you create your plan. Here is some what you'll learn:

— Three things I wish I knew before I started my business
— Strategies for re-activating distributors who have slowed down or quit
— Why you only need a FEW leaders to build a HUGE business (and where to find them)
— The truth about training, game plans, and working with distributors
— What to do when your team won't return your calls
— Techniques for getting your team to increase recruiting and production
— Multilevel marketing math (and how to use it to keep distributors from quitting)
— How to motivate unmotivated distributors—the secret used by top income earners
— No team? No problem. Here's what to do to get some
— How to get new distributors started right—without being a babysitter
— How to find "hidden gems" in your genealogy
— The one thing you should NEVER do with your team (Don't make the mistake I made)
— How to dramatically increase your odds of success

One thing you won't get in this book is a lot of hand holding. I'm not a cheerleader. You won't hear a motivational pep talk.

Instead, you'll learn specific strategies and techniques you can start using immediately, to get your team recruiting, selling, and growing.

You can fix your business. Turn to the next page and let me help.

David M. Ward

P.S. Join my free recruiting tips newsletter at http://recruitandgrowrich.com/newsletter

3 things I wish I knew before I started my business

Although my meeting with Ron lasted only a few minutes, what he told me about network marketing had a profound influence on me and my business. Hearing what Ron said lifted a heavy weight off of my shoulders because I realized that the "problems" I was having were normal and with some minor changes, I could fix things.

Yes, I wished I had been told these things when I started my business. I might have avoided some of my mistakes and not been so hard on myself.

On the other hand, maybe I needed to learn these things the hard way, through experience.

Either way, I was relieved to know that network marketing does work and I hadn't destroyed my business. In fact, I was on my way to building a very successful business. Here are the three things Ron told me.

(1) You only need a few

I thought Ron would ask questions about who I was recruiting, my approach, training, and so on, but he didn't. Instead, he said something I will never forget. He said that what I was experiencing was completely normal because statistically speaking, most people you sign up in the business do little or nothing.

I knew, of course, that most people you approach say no to the business. I'd had my share of those. But I always figured that most people who sign up would do something.

They paid money, they ordered product, they wanted to make a change in their life. How could they not at least try?

More importantly, how can anyone build a successful business if most people do little or nothing?

"Because you only need a few people who do something," Ron said, "a few leaders who get to work and build the business".

Ron explained that in network marketing, eighty to eighty-five percent do nothing, fifteen to twenty percent do a little, and three to five percent build a big business. "Those are your leaders," he said. " If you have a few of them, they can make you rich."

Just as you have to talk to a lot of prospects to get some to sign up, you have to sign up a lot of distributors to find leaders who will do that. But you only need a few.

He told me I was doing better than most. I was still very new in the business and I needed to give it more time.

He told me not to worry about the people who don't do anything. He said I should keep recruiting and I would eventually find my leaders.

Then he told me about his organization. He had thousands of distributors, he said, and most of them were also doing little or nothing.

He said that he's earning more than I was because he has more zeros in his genealogy—more people who are doing nothing. Although he had thousands of people on his team, only a few hundred were working the business.

But this was enough, he said, for him to consistently earn a high six-figure income. He said that all of the big-money earners have the same thing going on in their organizations.

You have no idea how excited I was to hear this. I had been blaming myself for having all those "zeros," not realizing that this was normal and that the more zeros I had, the more people I would have that were recruiting and producing.

I need to go get more zeros!

Later, I asked my upline about this. He agreed that most people do little or nothing, and that it didn't matter. At the time, he was earning $20,000 a month and had thousands of people who were doing nothing.

"Why didn't you tell me this when I was getting started?" I asked him. He said that most leaders don't tell new distributors this because they don't want to scare them. If they knew that most people do little or nothing, they might get discouraged and quit."

Discouraged? Not me. I thought it was one of the most exciting things I'd ever heard.

Let it go

Before I learned this, I did something I think many people do: I pushed my team. I called them and tried to get them to do something. I sent them more tools. I repeatedly reminded them about the calls and the events. I offered to make calls with them. I asked about their progress and repeatedly told them what they needed to do.

I pushed and pushed, but all I did was make things worse.

During our brief meeting, Ron told me to let go of my "need" to have my team doing something. "Don't push them," he said, "because when you push people, they back away".

Instead of pushing them, create an environment that encourages them to come to you. Let them know you're available to help them, stay in touch with them, keep them informed about what you and others are doing, but otherwise, leave them alone.

The ones who are ready to do something will do it and come to you if they need help.

Boom! Another revelation. Another dose of relief.

I was spending so much time and mental energy trying to get my team to do something and getting more and more frustrated. What a relief to know that I could let it go.

At the time, I hadn't heard about the Law of Attraction. I didn't know that we attract what we think about, so I didn't realize that by focusing on all of the people in my organization who weren't doing anything, all I was doing was attracting more people like them.

Don't laugh. That's exactly what was happening. I was constantly thinking about how much "wasted talent" I had on my team, thinking about who wasn't working and what I should do about it, and things were getting worse.

Ron told me to let it go. Emotionally detach from my need for them to do anything and let things happen naturally.

Help them get started. Let them know you're available to help them. Stay in touch with them. Promote to them. But never push them.

He also told me that I shouldn't assume they want what I want, even if they said they do. Let them do what they want to do, when (and if) they want to do it.

Ron said he focuses on the distributors in his organization who are working or who say they are ready to work and want his help. He told me to do the same.

"If you only have one or two people who are ready to work," he said, "that's who you should focus on."

(2) Work with the Willing

Ron told me that if I let go of the distributors who aren't doing anything, it not only frees up your mind, it frees up your calendar. Instead of trying to babysit your team, you can use that time to work with the ones who want your help.

He told me to "work with the willing" and forget about everyone else.

It's the same thing we do when we're recruiting. We sort through a list of prospects, looking for the ones who are interested and we let go of anyone who isn't. We don't try to talk anyone into signing up. We move on.

We should do the exact same thing when they sign up as a distributor.

Ron asked me if I had anyone in my organization who was doing anything, or had ever done anything. I thought about it and realized that yes, I did have a few people who had recruited one or two people and put some sales on the books.

He told me that those are the ones I should pay attention to and work with. But he also pointed out that my genealogy didn't tell the whole story.

"Your genealogy might have a bunch of zeros in the results column, but it doesn't tell you who might be doing the activities but not yet getting results," he said. "Some people may be making calls and showing up at events but you wouldn't know that just by looking at their numbers."

I had to admit that this was true.

"They may need more training or more time," he said, "but if they're trying, they deserve your attention."

But how do you know if someone is trying?

You ask them.

Ron said I needed to "take inventory". He told me to call everyone in my organization and find out who wants to work. Find out what they are doing and what they are willing to do.

Are they making calls? Listening to the team calls? Going to the weekly event?

If they're doing anything, even if they tell you they *plan* to do something, they should get some of your time.

Call everyone and find out who wants to work (or is working) and offer to help them.

And that's what I did.

I approached it the same way I approached recruiting. I didn't try to convince anyone to do anything. I didn't care whether someone was or wasn't interested, I just wanted an answer. Yes, they're ready to work or no, they aren't.

"Tell me yes, or tell me no, but tell me quick, I've got to go!"

If they didn't take my call, I left a message. If they didn't call me back, I knew they weren't ready to work the business, or if they were, they didn't want my help. Either way, I could stop calling them and move on.

Doing this allowed me to "eliminate" about half of the organization.

It didn't matter why they didn't talk to me or call me back. If they didn't want my help, if they were too busy for the business, if they had changed their mind, whatever it was, it didn't matter. It was one less distributor for me to worry about.

When I spoke to someone, I asked how things were going for them in the business. I asked if they had been to the latest event, or I told them about the next one. I shared a story or two about distributors in the company who were having success, to see if that might spark their interest. And I told me them how I was doing.

I tried to get a sense of whether or not they were still interested in the business and if they were doing (or planned to do) anything to move forward.

I also told them that I was available to help them and asked if they wanted to schedule time for some training, to go over their list, or have me help them make some calls.

If they showed some life, I worked with them. If they didn't, or if we set an appointment to talk again and they stood me up, I let them go.

I was done chasing anyone or trying to convince them that they "should" work the business. And it felt great.

Even greater, when I was done calling through the organization, I had found a few people who wanted to work with me. I let go of everyone who didn't want my help and focused on those few.

Those few, and few others who came later, eventually helped me build a huge organization.

I did stay in touch with everyone else, however, mostly by email. I shared news and success stories, promoted upcoming events, and offered encouragement. I also let them know that I was available to help.

If I knew them personally, I might occasionally call and say hello.

But that's it. No pressure. Just saying hi.

If they called me or emailed me to ask a question or for help, I helped them.

Other than that, I left them alone.

Taking Inventory

Taking inventory means calling everyone to find a few. A few who are serious. A few who are ready to work. A few who want to take their business to the next level.

With a small team, call everyone yourself. (When your team is bigger, ask your leaders to call through their organizations).

Start at the bottom of each leg. If you know them, tell them the purpose of your call (see below).

If you don't know them, introduce yourself and let them know that you are a part of their upline support team. Briefly tell them your story—your background, why you got started in the business, and what you want to accomplish or what you have accomplished so far.

Then, ask them to tell you about themselves. What's their background? Why did they get started in the business? What do they want to accomplish?

You want to know their "why"—their motivation.

If they're new, you might ask them a "getting started" question:

— Have you been to the "Getting Started" training yet?
— Has your sponsor done a "game plan" with you yet?
— Have you ordered product/tools?
— Have you set up your website?
— Have you scheduled your [launch event]?
— How far along are you on making your list?
— Do you have questions for me about the business?

You might also ask them if they have any previous experience with network marketing. Their answer may help you to do a better job of helping them.

Listen to what they say and how they say it. Whether they're new or they have been in the business for months or years, you're looking for people who are excited about the business, committed to it, willing to learn and willing to take action.

If you know them, you can say, " I'm just checking in," or, "I thought I'd give you a quick call and see how things are going." Ask them about their goals for the month. If they don't have a goal or they say they "need to think about it," ask if they would like to do a new "game plan" with you, to set some goals and a plan to achieve them.

Give every distributor you speak with your contact information and tell them what to do to take the next step. (We'll talk about that in later chapters.)

Next, call their immediate upline and do the same thing. Tell them you've spoken with the distributor (or distributors) under them and they're ready to get started (or take their business to the next level).

If a distributor you spoke to didn't sound excited about the business, find something positive you can say about them. Perhaps they know a lot of people. They might have business or sales experience. Maybe they've signed up for the next training or ordered product or tools.

Ask the upline how they know or recruited the distributor(s) under them. If the distributor(s) under them are new, ask the upline what have they done with them, e.g., game plan, launch event, training, etc.

Tell the upline that you are excited to work with them and their team and to let you know what you can do to help. Even better, suggest something you can do, such as making some calls with them. If they're open to that, schedule a date and time.

After that, call *their* upline and do the same thing. Keep going up the line, all the way to your front line distributor.

Doing it this way, from the bottom up, allows you to light a fire under the distributors in a leg. They may have never talked to their downline themselves and may not realize that they have some people under them who are ready to get to work. They might be encouraged by your positive report, motivated to work with their team and motivated to get to work themselves.

Your objective is to identify those distributors who are ready to get to work. It doesn't matter how much or how little they've done before, what matters is that they are ready to start or re-start their business and are open to your help.

You might have only one or two who fit this description, but they are the ones you work with.

Take inventory of your team on a regular basis, say every three to six months. Doing this will help you find new people to work with, including distributors who weren't ready to get to work the last time you spoke to them but are ready now.

As your team grows, you'll want to have additional ways to take inventory so you can separate out those who truly are ready from those who merely say they are. I'll show you how to do that later in this book.

(3) The power of "one"

The third thing Ron told me that had a profound impact on my business had to do with recruiting. Ron said I should continue to "go wide," that is, recruit as many "front line" distributors as I could, to add profitability and replace the ones who weren't working. "Recruit to replace," he called it. (Note: your comp plan may be different; check with your upline or company.)

Don't worry about the ones who aren't working, Ron said. Go get some more.

Later, at a convention, another leader put it this way: "If you can't change your people, change your people".

Ron also told me that in addition to going wide, I needed to "go deep". He said that the strength of your organization lies in how deep it is. A leader is only a leader when they have other leaders under them. A leg isn't a leg until it has other legs under it.

I had assumed that this would occur naturally. Ron said it would, "but if you're smart, you won't depend on that."

He told me to work with the distributors under me, no matter how deep they are, and help them recruit. Don't assume they will do it, or that anyone else in their upline will help them.

It's your business. You do it.

He said that in addition to driving depth in my organization this way, **I would never run out of prospects to talk to**.

Every distributor knows people you don't know. **Every distributor can lead you to at least one new distributor.**

Help them recruit one, then work with that new distributor to recruit one. Keep going until you (or they) recruit someone who goes to work on their own.

It's called "the power of one" and it's one of the most important concepts in network marketing.

The conduit theory

The fact that every distributor can recruit at least one person changed the way I looked at this business. It allowed me to drive depth in my organization and it can do the same for yours.

Most network marketing experts tell you that training your team is the key to success. It is important, of course, and we'll talk about training in an upcoming chapter. But let's face it, you could train a distributor until you're blue in the face and they still might do nothing.

Therefore, as important as training is, when working with your team, your number one objective shouldn't be training. Your number one objective should be to **recruit someone they know**.

This means looking at your distributors as a conduit to their prospects. Who do they know? Who can they lead you to?

Work with your distributors and help them recruit someone they know. *Or get their list and recruit them yourself.*

You have a business to build and the main function of that business is bringing in new people (and the sales that come with them). If your distributors won't do it (and you have to assume that they won't because, statistically speaking most people do little or nothing), *you* need to do it.

I call this, "the conduit theory". Every distributor you work with, whether you recruit them yourself or someone on your team recruits them, is a gateway or conduit to other people.

If you adopt this strategy to build your business, it opens up a lot of possibilities. It won't matter if a prospect on your list isn't right for the business or doesn't have leadership potential. It won't matter if they work slowly or not at all.

These things don't matter because it's not about them, **it's about who they know**. Recruit someone they know so that when the distributor drops out you'll have someone new to work with. Do the same thing with the distributors they lead you to. Continue doing that until you have someone, perhaps many levels deep in your organization, who starts building a team.

You can do this with every distributor on your team, including the ones who aren' t doing anything and don't plan to. You can tell them, "Give me your list and I'll help you get your team started."

Go recruit one or two people on their list and work with them.

Lather, rinse, repeat.

You can even use this in your own "front line" recruiting.

Let's say you're speaking to someone who hesitates to sign up because they "don't have the time".

Make them an offer: "Introduce me to one or two people who might be interested in building a business/earning more income. I'll recruit them and put them under you."

You can do the same thing with referrals. Your Uncle Henry might tell you he's not interested in the business but he is willing to give you a few names of people he knows who might be interested. If you recruit them, you can go back to your Uncle and offer to put his friend(s) under him.

If he says yes, great. If he says no, it's still great because he led you to people you didn't know and might never have met. *They* might be the leader you're looking for, or lead you to them.

This is network marketing at it's core. People leading you to people. And everyone can lead to you to at least one.

Getting your team to suit up and get in the game

Why is it that so many distributors never get started? Why do so many quit?

It's not the company or the products. It's not the training. It's not you.

The reason so many people give up before they even start is fear.

Fear of being rejected by friends and family, fear of talking to strangers, fear of failure, and even fear of success. Fear is an extraordinarily powerful emotion that has destroyed the dreams of countless distributors.

But there is an antidote to fear: belief.

When a distributor believes that they can succeed, they will do something many distributors don't do: they'll try. They may be scared, they may not know what to do, they may not be good, but they'll do *something*, which is always better than doing nothing.

With belief they have a chance. Without belief it doesn't matter how much training they get, how great your products are or how much your comp plan pays. If they don't believe they can be successful, they'll never get started, or if they do, it won't take much to knock them out.

As a friend of mine puts it, "an ounce of doubt and you're out".

One of the most important things you can do when working with your team is to help them develop their belief—in the company, the products or services, the network marketing business model, in you and their upline support team, and most importantly, belief in themselves.

There is a sort of invisible line in network marketing. On one side of the line are new distributors, most of whom don't yet have that belief. They're excited but scared. They hope they can do it but they're not sure.

They've signed up, they're in the business, but the business isn't in them. Not yet, anyway.

On the other side of the line are distributors who do believe. They've had some positive results and they're hungry for more. The things they feared weren't as bad as they imagined. They've done enough to know that they can make it and they're willing to keep at it until they do.

Whether they are new or newly re-engaging, your job is to help your distributors across that line. To help them conquer their doubts and fears and develop their belief.

Skin in the game

One of the first things you should do is to make sure they have some "skin in the game". That means taking steps to get them to invest in their business so that they have something to lose if they don't move forward.

Most network marketing companies today require very little money to become a distributor. If you've got only $25 invested in your new business, or even a few hundred dollars, it's not difficult to walk away. They haven't really lost anything.

If they invest more than a small amount, walking away isn't as easy. If they have more to lose than the price of a meal, they are more likely to try harder and stick around longer.

Their investment in the business isn't only measured in money, however. It's also a function of their reputation, pride, and feeling of self-worth.

When I started in a network marketing company many years ago, my start-up costs were around $600 and that didn't include inventory. I could afford the start-up fees (and the $5,000 I later paid for inventory), and I could afford to walk away from my investment if it didn't pan out, but the possibility of losing my investment weighed heavily on my mind.

After I got started and went to a couple of events, I had doubts about the business. I thought it wasn't right for me. I thought I wouldn't have time to do it. I had lots of reasons to quit the business, but I didn't want to admit to myself (or my wife) that I had lost $600.

I decided that I was not going to lose that investment, that I would do whatever it took to earn at least that much and "break even".

I asked my sponsor what I had to do to earn back the $600, got to work and made it happen.

I'm not suggesting that you encourage distributors to spend thousands of dollars on inventory or tools or leads or anything they can't afford. But you should encourage them to invest a bit more than they might otherwise do on their own.

They need to stretch. They need to be committed to the business.

Get them to buy something or do something so that they have some skin in the game so that it's harder for them to quit than to move forward.

On a side note, if a distributor won't invest in their business, it tells you something about how much time you should spend investing in them.

In my business, if a distributor won't buy our product, I won' work with them. I know they aren't going to be successful if they don't believe enough in what we're doing to purchase it themselves. "When someone asks you how it has worked for you, what are you going to say?" I'll ask them.

If a distributor won't buy your product, get some tools or leads or sign up for the web site, if they won't invest time coming to the training and getting on the calls, you might want to back off and work with someone else.

Unless you find another way to get them across the line.

Get them trained (again)

Prior to being trained, distributors often imagine that the business will be complicated and difficult. After training, they usually see that they "can do this".

They may be scared, they may need practice, they may need help, but what once seemed nearly impossible to them is now something they can see themselves doing.

Get them to the "getting started" training and their confidence and belief will grow.

Get them to the training more than once because it has a cumulative effect. The first time you see a training, you don't grasp everything. The information comes at you quickly and when something new is presented, you may still be thinking about the previous idea. The next time you go to the training, you "hear" things you didn't hear before.

If repetition is the mother of learning, it is the father of building confidence and belief.

Each time they go to a training, they see and hear the information "in context". They've actually tried some of the things they are hearing. They can visualize themselves doing them again and getting better results.

Get your distributors trained and encourage them to go to the training again, even if it is the same basic training. Go with them, to set an example, and encourage them to bring their new (or re-engaging) distributors with them.

Training builds confidence and helps distributors cross the line to belief.

Get them to the events

Do whatever you can do to get your distributors to come to the next presentation. Live events have energy and excitement and your distributors can easily get caught up in that.

Live events have speakers who know how to present the facts in a compelling way. They have powerful stories about the products and how they have changed lives. They have stories about people on their team who are making their dreams come true.

Get your distributors to come to the next event. It's one of the most important things you can do to help them cross the line.

At the event, introduce them to other distributors who will welcome them, share their stories, and make them feel like they are among friends. Your distributor will meet other distributors who overcame the same doubts and fears that are holding them back and went on to great success. They might hear just the right story that captures their heart and inspires them to do more.

This is just as true for new distributors as for re-engaging distributors who need another dose of the excitement that captivated them when they first got started.

At the event, your distributors will hear about the next event and why they need to attend. Going to that next event will get them to go to the one after that.

Get your team into the habit of going to all the events. It will keep them in the business until they overcome most of their fears and doubts, get some positive results, and build their belief that they really can be successful.

Tell their story

Another thing you can do to build their belief is to tell their story. Once you know why they started their business, you need to continually remind them of their "why".

Did they start because they're always working and don't have time for their kids? Did they start because they want to help their parents retire? Did they start because they want to see the world but don't have the time or the money?

Whatever their story, keep it in front of them. Remind them why they started the business and that all of their effort will be worth it.

When they get their first check or direct deposit, remind them that they are on their way to accomplishing their goal. When they have a bad week or month and seem to be in danger of slipping away, bring them back by reminding them of what they said they want to accomplish.

You should also tell their story when you introduce them to other distributors. "John, this is Mary. She just signed up and wants to earn enough to quit her job and start a family."

Every time Mary hears you say this to others she is reminded about what's at stake. Make sure you tell her about (and introduce her to) other distributors who have been able to do what she wants to do. Their stories will encourage Mary and help her to believe that if they can do it, she can do it too.

Get them to "go public"

One of the first things new real estate agents and insurance agents do is notify everyone in their warm market about their new business. They send an email or make a call or stick something in the mail, and it's done. They've made the announcement and they can move forward.

Most people don't buy anything from one email or letter, but at least they know what the new agent is doing, making it easier for the agent to contact them again to schedule an appointment or offer more information.

In network marketing, fear stops many new distributors from telling their friends and family about their new business. They don't want to be laughed at, told they're going to fail, or hear "those things never work". If they've been in network marketing before, they don't want people to remind them that it didn't work the last time they tried it.

But most of this fear is in their minds and blown out of proportion. The sooner they "come out" and tell their friends and family what they're doing, the sooner they will see that most people don't laugh at them or tell them they've joined a cult.

Help your distributor understand the value of "going public" about their new business and encourage them to do it. Let them know they don't have to offer their products or opportunity, just let people know what they're doing.

Once the cat is out of the bag, there's nothing left to fear. Everyone knows what they are doing and the world hasn't ended. And, by telling everyone what they're doing, it is very likely that some of those people will be interested in hearing something about what they're doing.

Once they make a sale or recruit a distributor, nobody will be able to tell them, "the business doesn't work". They've already seen that it does.

Get them to use the product(s)

Distributors need to get excited about the products or services they represent. They need to feel that everyone needs to know about them and what they can do. They obviously can't do that unless and until they've used the products or services themselves.

Encourage them to use the product and tell you what they think.

When they report to you about their experience, you can share how you and others have used and benefited from the products. If they have any questions or issues with a product, you can address these before they speak to anyone else.

Getting them to use the products not only helps them get comfortable with the products and how to use them, it gives them a personal "product story" they can share with their prospects. Telling that story, sharing their positive experience, is a great way to build their own belief in the products. It's also a great way to get their prospects to buy something.

Show them what's possible

One way I've found to build a distributor's belief in the business is to talk to them about the people on their list.

I look at 10 or 20 names and have them tell me something about those people. I try to have something positive to say about at least a few of those prospects. I tell my distributor that I'm excited about them and what they can do in the business.

I'll usually zero in on professionals or business owners or anyone with network marketing or sales experience. If a prospect knows a lot of people, I' ll talk about how they might be able to recruit a lot of them, sell a lot of product, or both.

When I get excited about the people on their list, they usually get excited, too.

Another thing I do is tell my distributor about other distributors in our company who have been successful. I tell their stories, which always have a happy ending, and show my distributor "what's possible" in this business.

This is especially effective when the successful distributors you talk about come from a similar background to your distributor, or to the people on their list.

If your distributor is a real estate agent, or knows a lot of real estate agents, for example, pointing out successful real estate agents in your company shows your distributor that they can be successful approaching the real estate agents they know.

Get them on the phone

For a new distributor, the heaviest object in the universe is the phone. They often have trouble picking it up and making those first few calls.

And yet they must.

If you leave it to them to do, there's a good chance it won"t happen. So don't leave it to them. Do it with them.

Coach them on what to say and sit with them while they make the calls. Or have them call their prospects, introduce you, and listen to you do the exposure or make the invitation. This can be done in person or via 3-way calls.

Once they see that someone they know said, "Yes, I'd like to look at some information," or, "Sure, I'll come to that event," their confidence will grow and they'll be a big step closer to doing it themselves.

Show them how to do things the right way. Stay close to them and help them get some yeses under their belt.

You might start out by letting your distributors listen to you making first calls and follow-up calls to your prospects. Do this with re-engaging distributors, too, who may have done it wrong in the past, or not done it at all.

Get them some results

In network marketing we often say that your first check is your "belief" check. It proves to the new distributor that the business works. Stick close to your distributors and help them get that first check. It's the best thing you can do to help them cross the line.

That belief check also helps them create a story they can tell their prospects and team.

When they can say, "I've only been doing this for a week and I've already earned $200 and gotten my first business partner," not only will they have a story they can use to recruit others, their confidence and belief will grow because they're also telling this story to themselves.

But don't stop there. Keep working with them and their new distributors and help your distributor get their first *override*.

Because while a distributor's first check is their belief check, their first check that contains overrides is the one that will truly build their belief in the business and get them across the line.

The truth about training

Once you've taken inventory and found some people who are ready to work, the next step is to sit down with them and do a "game plan" just as you would do if they were new. Spend an hour finding out what they want to achieve in the business and then show them what they need to do to get it.

If you haven't talked about it yet, the first part of the game plan is to find out their "why".

Why did they get started? What do they want to accomplish short term? Where do they want to be in five years?

What's painful in their life right now? What do they want to eliminate or change? What keeps them up at night?

You need to know why they signed up so that you can remind them of their why if you see their numbers dropping or they start expressing doubts about the business. Knowing their why allows you to show them what they're working for and why it's worth the effort. It also helps you to create a plan for them.

Don't assume they want what you want. You need to know what *they* want. You may have set your sights on earning $5,000 per month while they may be happy to earn a few hundred dollars per month, at least for now. These are very different goals and require very different levels of activity. Help them create a plan that will help them achieve their goals.

You can do another plan later, when their goals have changed.

Once you know what they want, talk to them about what they're willing to do to get it. If they want to earn $5,000 per month starting in 90 days, but they're only willing to work 30 minutes a day, you need to explain to them that there is a mismatch between what they want and what they're willing to do. Help them understand that to achieve that goal, they need to

(a) invest more time in the business,
(b) extend the deadline,
(c) reduce their goal,

. . .or some combination of the above.

If they have unreasonable expectations about the business, it's going to be difficult to work with them. They're going to quickly become disillusioned and frustrated and be more likely to drop out.

You have to be honest with them about what it will take to reach their goals, and they have to be honest with you about what they're willing to do to reach them. Once you have an understanding, you can move forward.

If they're a new distributor, the next step is to give them the information they will need to build the business, or show them where to find it, e.g., on the company website or in their distributor kit. This information will include some (but not necessarily all) of the following:

— Events/calendar. Make sure they know about the live events in their area, as well as the events that take place online and via conference call. Include business presentations, trainings, team calls, company calls, and so on.

They may not be ready for everything but they need to know where to find out what's available.

At the very least, let them know about the *next* event, whether that's a business overview, a training, a Super Saturday, or your team call. Tell them that it is important for them to be there and ask for their commitment. If they're local, offer to pick them up.

— Tools. They need to know which tools are available. Tell them about the DVDs, web sites, recorded messages, and so on, and have them listen or watch all of them. Tell them the ones you use and recommend. Show them where to order them.

— Product knowledge. This should be covered in the company training but you may want to go over some of this with them, show them where they can get more information, and share a story or two that they can use when they're speaking with prospects.

— How to get their first/next promotion. Don't go over the entire comp plan with them but do make sure they know what they need to do to get to the next level.

— Their back office. If your company provides distributors with a back office that includes stats, forms, a calendar and other resources, help them get registered and give them a quick tour.

— The system. Make sure they know the recruiting system used by you and your team. Make sure they know how to approach and expose prospects, follow-up, and close. You won't have time to go over everything, but at least make sure they know there is a system and why they should follow it.

— Their support team. Make sure the have contact information for their upline support team. Tell them something about the individuals who can help them. After the game plan, introduce them to their upline, and to others on the team who can welcome them, share an inspiring story, and promote the next event.

— 3-way calling. One of the most important elements in working with your team is the 3-way call. It allows a brand new distributor to start getting results almost immediately. You want them to see that they don't need to know that much to get started, they can call their support team and have someone else answer their prospect's questions and close them or move them to the next step.

Of course we also use 3-way calls to welcome new distributors to the team, to promote events, for training, and for otherwise supporting and working with upline and downline distributors. During the game plan, you won't have time to teach them everything about 3-way calls. But you should make sure they have 3-way calling capability on their phone(s) and that they know how to use it.

Note, there is a detailed discussion of how to make 3-way calls (what to say, what to do, as both the distributor with a prospect and as their "expert") in my other book, *Recruit and Grow Rich*.

Most of your game plan should be spent going over their list. If they don't have a list, help them start one. If they have very few names on their list, help them expand it. They need prospects to talk to. They haven't started (or re-started) their business until they have a list.

Make sure they know not to contact anyone until they've had some training and/or until you can be there with them in person or on the phone to show them what to do.

What if they aren't new?

If they aren't a new distributor, if they know most or all of the above, work with them to create a plan that is appropriate to their experience, results, skills, and knowledge.

You might start with something called a **S. W. O. T. Analysis**.

S. W. O. T. stands for "Strengths, Weaknesses, Opportunities, and Threats". It is used in the business and corporate world to asses the current condition of a business and help plan its future.

Ask you distributor to asses themselves:

What are their **STRENGTHS**?

What are they good at? What do they like? What comes easily to them?

This may include the tools and approaches they like to use, lead generation methods, types of prospects they relate to, and more. They may be good at speaking, doing three-way calls as an "expert," overcoming objections, closing, or training. They may be good writers, or have great organizational sills. They may be good at promoting or know how to run a meeting.

Ask questions to prompt them. Share your thoughts and observations about them. Have them write down everything, and make sure you get a copy.

Next, ask them to describe their **WEAKNESSES**.

What do they struggle with? What intimidates or frightens them? If they had a choice, what would they prefer not doing?

They might uncomfortable on the phone. They may not have enough prospects. They might have less time for the business than is needed to reach their goals.

They may not be good at getting prospects to look at the presentation. They may not be good at follow-up. They may be shy or have difficulty promoting or leading their team.

If their upline doesn't help them, or gives them bad advice, that's a weakness.

They may not be able to invest a lot of money in inventory, training, leads, or web sites.

They may have problems with their self-image, confidence, or belief in the products.

Again, have them put this in writing. This will allow you to help them improve or find someone in your upline who can do that.

Next on the list is to identify their **OPPORTUNITIES**.

These may overlap with some of their strengths. Opportunities might include people they know but haven't approached, a source of high quality leads or lists, or having an upline who is willing to go out of their way to help them make calls or coach them.

Opportunities may also include personal contacts who are willing to introduce them to prospects, promote their products to their clients or customers, allow them to do a guest post on their blog, or let them use their conference room for sit-downs or trainings.

Finally, what **THREATS** do they face?

Threats might include family or friends who discourage or disparage them, distributors who are stealing their prospects, a job that is too far away from their weekly event (so they often arrive late), or a lack of local events (or good events) in their market or a market where they have team.

By doing a S. W. O. T. Analysis, they will be able to take an objective look at where they are in the business and what they need to do to improve. You can then help them maximize their strengths, minimize or eliminate their weaknesses, exploit their opportunities, and overcome any threats.

One or more of these issues may be what held them back in the past. By working through them, you can help your distributor effectively start over and increase their odds of success.

To do this, you can offer advice, recommend training and resources, or introduce them to other distributors who might help them overcome a challenge by sharing how they dealt with it themselves.

If they need more prospects, you can talk to them about ways to expand their warm market list and their options for recruiting in the cold market.

If they need help with approaching prospects, go over the approaches and scripts, role play, and get on the phone with them.

Whatever you do, you should be encouraging. Tell them they can solve that problem or improve that skill and tell them you'll do whatever you can to help them do that.

Don't end the game plan or meeting without promoting the next step, whether that's the next business overview or team call, getting together with you to make calls, going to the training, conducting their private business reception or launch party, or doing a conference call with their team, perhaps with you as the guest speaker.

The game plan will obviously depend on many factors, including how long they've been in the business. If they're getting re-started after six months of inaction, for example, you'll need to bring them up to date and regarding company news and upcoming events. If they never learned the right way to do the business, you ' ll want to start from scratch and get them properly trained.

If they've been around for awhile and made mistakes, don't dwell on those mistakes. Focus on what they need to do to move forward, not what they should not have done in the past. John C. Maxwell said, "You don't change people by telling them they are wrong, you change them by showing them there is a better way".

I realize that your company or team (or you) may do things differently. You may utilize "game plan" time with new distributors to actually do exposures. That's fine. Just make sure you do the other parts at some point.

After the game plan

Zig Ziglar was speaking about network marketing when he said, "The only thing worse than training someone and having them leave is to not train them and have them stay."

And it's true. Because training is essential to success in network marketing.

Think about it, most new distributors have little or no experience in network marketing. They don't have a sales or business background. They don't know what to do or how to do it.

Worse, they do have network marketing experience but they were given bad information or they were poorly trained and don't know how to build a successful business.

It's up to you to show them, and to stick close to them until they can do it without you.

If you recruited them yourself, you showed them how to approach and expose a prospect by what you said and did with them. Review what you did with them and encourage them to do the same things with their prospects. If you didn't follow the system, however, make sure you point out your errors and explain why they *shouldn't* do what you did.

Make sure they understand the concept of duplication and the importance of using tools and events to do exposures. Make sure they know the importance of getting prospects on the phone with you or another distributor, instead of answering their prospect's questions themselves.

Now, this doesn't mean you should do all of their training. There isn't time to train everyone who joins your team. You need to spend most of your time recruiting new distributors.

The solution is to use use your team and company training and materials for most of the training. Your job is to point to that training, promote the value of attending it, and then reinforce what they have learned with your words and by showing them what you do.

By doing this, you're also showing them what they should do to get their new distributors started. They can duplicate what you did with them, and their new recruits can do the same.

Don't smother your babies in their crib

Whether you're training a new distributor or working with someone who is getting re-engaged, one thing to keep in mind is that many distributors are fragile. It doesn't take much to overwhelm them.

When I was new, I made the mistake of giving my new recruits too much information. I spent hours training them. I sent them a big box of every tool the company had. I asked them to attend not just the next event but every event on the calendar. I told them that if they didn't do everything, they weren't going to be successful. (Yikes!)

Looking back, I'm surprised anybody did anything.

By contrast, the distributors in our company who had flourishing businesses focused less on giving their distributors information and more on getting them into action.

They gave their new distributors only enough information to get them started, and then helped them do the activities and get some results.

After my talk with Ron, I realized that I had unreasonable expectations about my team and was asking too much of them. I switched gears. I cut the game plan down to under an hour. I sent them only a few tools. I made sure they knew where the training or the next event was taking place and encouraged them to go.

I went over their list with them, made calls with them and helped them to do some exposures. I coached them on what to say. I encouraged them to introduce me to their prospects so I could answer their questions and help them get signed up.

Once they started getting results (signing up distributors, getting promoted, making money, etc.), they got excited and wanted to learn more and do more.

Don't overwhelm your new or newly re-engaging distributors with too much information or too much training. Give them only enough to get them started. Focus on activity, not information, and you'll be amazed at how quickly your business can grow.

The truth about duplication

The first rule of working with distributors is to set a good example for them. Always do what you want them to do because they will do what you do, not what you say they should do.

That means consistently following the system used by your company or team.

In fact, at the end of each day, ask yourself, "If my team did what I did today, would my business grow?" If you don't like the answer, you have work to do.

Your team learns by watching you. If you show them that you are casual about the business, not working it consistently, not going to the events, not on the team calls, and so on, you shouldn't be surprised that they aren't, either.

If distributors call you during the work day to ask questions or chat and you take their call, the message you convey is that it's okay to chat during work hours (and it is not). They need to be told that during work hours, they can call you to introduce you to a prospect or a new distributor, but for anything else, (questions, reporting results, problems, etc.), they should call after work hours.

Of course you need to do the same. You shouldn't call them to chat or see how they're doing during work hours. During work hours, you are working and they should be, too.

Your ideal distributor

Take a moment to think about your ideal distributor—the type of person you would like to have on your team.

How do they spend their day? How much activity do they do? What kind of goals do they set? What kind of results do they tend to get?

What are their attitudes and beliefs about the business? How do they handle problems? How do they help their team?

Once you have a picture of your ideal distributor, write it down. And then begin working on *becoming* that distributor because you don't necessarily attract what you want, you attract what you are.

If you want to bring in a certain type of distributor—hard working, focused, committed, positive, determined, and so on—that's who you must become.

Because like attracts like.

And here's the thing—you can't fake it. You can't pretend. You have to follow the system you want your team to follow even if your team can't see or hear you, because somehow they know.

They know what you're not doing because your activity or lack thereof reveals itself in the things you say and don't say. When you talk about the events, for example, they know if you are going. When everyone is talking about and excited about the convention and you don't mention it (because you're not going), they can tell. If you aren't sharing stories with them about the exposures you're doing and the results you're getting, they know you're not doing exposures or getting results.

And they will do what you do.

It's not that you have to be the perfect distributor in all things and at all times. But you have to try, especially when it comes to the basics. Do your best to always follow the system, because you will duplicate yourself whether you want to or not.

You also have to protect your team from bad ideas and habits of other distributors. Your team will be influenced by what they see other distributors do and what they hear at the trainings and on conference calls.

They will be tempted to take shortcuts. If someone else doesn't go the events, for example, and they seem to be having success, they will want to take those same shortcuts.

You must protect them.

Make sure they go to trainings that are consistent with the way you do business. Keep them away from events and distributors who do something else. Help them to understand that while some distributors don't follow the system and seem to be successful, they usually don't last long term.

Ask your upline to help you. Ask them to share some stories about distributors who made some money for a year or two and then were gone.

Do whatever you have to do to steer your team down the correct path. If you don't, they will either be confused about what to do or take the shortcuts that will eventually lead to failure.

Duplication starts with you. You do the activities (correctly), you teach it to your team (and model the correct behavior), they do what you do and then teach it to their team.

That's how a large team and a long-term business is built.

One person (you) becomes two. Two becomes four. Before you know it, there are hundreds on your team, on the way to becoming thousands. But that won't happen if you don't do it first.

Network marketing in general, and duplication in particular, is about systems. Individuals may come and go but faithful allegiance to the system is what keeps the business strong.

The goal is to get a large number of people to do a few simple things. You want everyone, prospects and distributors alike, to see that the you follow a simple system that anyone can follow. Because if they think they can't do what you're doing, most people won't even try.

There's an added benefit to you for consistently following that system: it forces you to maintain your own level of activity. You might feel like skipping a day but you don't do it because you want to set an example for your team.

The most successful people in network marketing are masters at keeping things simple. They focus on the basics, which account for 80 to 90% of their results.

You should do the same.

Master the basics, model the basics, and promote the basics to your team. Don't let anything else distract you.

Because duplication starts with you.

Get yourself out of the way

When you are training and working with your team, in addition to following the system you want them to follow, the best way to teach them that system is to get yourself out of the way and point to someone else.

They may be your upline or someone on your team. They could be anyone else in the company you know is faithful to the same system and consistently getting results.

Don't explain "the system," go with your team to the company or team training where it is taught.

Don't tell your team what you think, quote your upline leaders about what they have taught you.

Don't create your own tools or websites, or encourage your team to do that. Point to the company tools and websites and encourage your team to use them.

Don't talk about your achievements, talk about other distributors on your team, sideline or upline.

Show them that you follow the system, but don't make the system about you.

Point at other successful distributors who follow the system. Say nice things about them. Not only will your team learn better this way, they will be able to do the same thing with their teams.

Also, make sure you introduce your team to these other distributors. They may "click" with them more than they do with you. They may relate to their background, personality, or style.

One time, I signed up a certain distributor who wasn't reaching his potential. I had only spoken to him on the phone at that point but I could tell there was something holding him back.

I invited him to a presentation where I was the speaker. He told me he liked what he heard, but for some reason, he and I weren't on the same page. We went to dinner after the event where I introduced him to other distributors who were a better fit for his personality. He liked them a lot and sold himself on the business.

He went on to become a very successful distributor and a good friend.

Don't manage your team

Your job isn't to manage your team. They don't work for you. They don't want you telling them what to do. And even if they did, there's no way you could manage a team of thousands of people.

Your job is to recruit them and help them get their business started. After that, as their business grows, you support them because doing that helps your business grow.

Support means speaking to some of their prospects and closing them. Other ways to support your team including promoting the events to them, helping them invite guests, and praising and recognizing their achievements.

But you can only do so much. At some point, as your team gets bigger, you have to be more selective about who you help and how much time you give them. You'll never grow your team into the thousands if you insist on personally working with everyone.

Many network marketing trainings teach you to give your team, "unconditional support." Be there for them, do whatever you can to help them—no matter what.

But this is silly.

Nobody is entitled to your support simply because they are under you in the genealogy. If you signed them up, help them get started. Beyond that, work with and support those who EARN your support.

You run a business. You get to choose who you work with, and who you don't. If someone isn't working, if they aren't following the system, if they aren't getting any results, you don't have to work with them.

It's your business, after all. You get to decide how you spend your time.

I mentioned earlier what I do with distributors who don't buy product. I have a talk with them about why it is important and give them a chance to do the right thing. They usually do this on their own, once they realize that they're not going to get anyone to buy the product or become a distributor if they don't do it themselves.

When they don't figure this out, I stop working with them.

I know some leaders who refuse to work with anyone who doesn't buy a certain training program or sign up for the convention. They believe that distributors who won't do those things are unlikely to be successful and they don't want to waste their time working with people who are probably going to fail.

I don't go that far but I don't give them as much time as I give other distributors who show me they are committed to the business.

You can't make anybody do anything. So don't try. Instead, show them where you are going with the business and invite them to join you. Tell them you'll help them, as long as they follow the system and make an effort.

Show them the better future that's available to them and offer to help them get there. If they want to work with you, great. If they don't, wish them well, let them know you'll be available if things change for them, and then work with the ones who both want and deserve your help.

That's leadership, not management. That's how you build a successful business.

How to get your team to increase their numbers

Again, your job isn't to convince anyone to do anything. It is to identify the people on your team who *want* to build their business and are *willing* to do the work, and help *them*.

If they're new or were never properly trained, you help them to learn the system used by your company or team. You do a game plan, help them make a list, show them the tools, and teach them how to approach prospects.

You show them how to do a proper exposure and follow-up. You speak with their interested prospects, answer questions, overcome objections and close those prospects or invite them to take the next step.

In other words, you help your distributors get started and get some results.

But only if they want and deserve your help.

After that, you spend less time helping them learn and use the basics and more time as a leader, using some of the following strategies to inspire them to build *their* team and increase their team's recruiting and production.

Praise and recognition

When distributors sign up their first distributor, make a sale, get promoted, qualify for a bonus, or do anything positive, let them know that you noticed.

Praise them. Make a fuss. Make them feel good about themselves. Let them know you appreciate having them on your team.

Praise them verbally and via email. Recognize their accomplishments with a plaque or trophy, a book or other small gifts.

Recognize their achievements in front of other distributors—in your team circle-ups, on the team call, or by mentioning it when the two of you are in the company of other distributors. If those other distributors are also on your team, this has the added benefit of encouraging your other distributors to do more, so they too can be recognized in front of others.

But don't limit this to their accomplishments. Also praise and recognize their efforts. Go out of your way to find them doing something right.

Compliment them when they have guests at an event, share their testimonial from stage, or get mentioned on the team call. Praise them when they read the book you suggested to them or they show up at the event "looking sharp".

Say something nice about the way they told their story to someone else's guest. Tell everyone about how hard they're working and how you are certain they are on their way to building a big business.

When you praise and recognize someone's positive behavior, they feel good about themselves (and you) and they are more likely to repeat the behavior that earned that recognition.

They also learn what to do when someone on their team does something worthy of praise and recognition.

Keep them "close to the fire"

One of the best things you can do to get your team excited and motivated is to make sure they come to local events and especially the bigger regional events and conventions.

There is energy and excitement at the events they will never feel sitting in their home office. At the events, new products are revealed, company news is shared, and top distributors share their training methods and success stories. Your distributors meet other distributors, become inspired by them, and find workout partners and friends.

We're in the people business. Your distributors need to be around other distributors.

When they meet distributors they look up to, they will want to emulate them. When they meet successful distributors who are younger or have less experience in life or in business than they do, they will realize that they too can be successful.

And when they meet friends and neighbors at an event they didn't know were in the business, they will realize that if they don't get busy and approach everyone they know, someone else will sign them up!

Once a week, your team should be at their local event. That's where things are happening. That's where the fire is and you should keep your team close to that fire.

Whether that event is a business presentation or a training or team event, they need to be there. When they go to the weekly event, it sustains them for another week. If they are new or getting re-engaged, the weekly event will keep them going until they start making sales and signing up distributors.

Once they've signed up some distributors, they'll want to keep going to the events to set an example for their team, and to help their team grow *their* teams.

Distributors with the biggest teams aren't necessarily the biggest recruiters or producers. They are often the best promoters, however.

They know that the distributor who has the most "butts in seats" at the events will build the biggest teams and make the most money. They will, therefore, continually promote the events to their teams.

You should do the same.

Make sure your team knows that you are 100% committed to being at the events.

Call your local team team before each event, especially when they are new, and tell them you're looking forward to seeing them. Promote the speaker or trainer. Offer to help them invite guests.

After each event, in your "circle up" or team meeting, always promote the *next* event.

Accountability calls

When you have a few distributors who are ready to work, one way to keep them motivated is to invite them to an accountability call. Basically, that means getting on a conference call with you once a week (or more often if you want) and reporting two sets of numbers: what they did the previous week and what they plan to do in the coming week.

There is no training or socializing on the call. Everyone is there simply to report their numbers. As the leader, you go through the list of distributors who were invited on the call, ask each one for their report, and move on to the next one.

Their numbers should relate to their activities and/or results. These numbers serve as a way to measure their progress and hold themselves accountable to you and others on the call.

The numbers they report are often referred to as "Key Performance Indicators" (KPIs). They include things like the number of exposures they did, the number of guests they had at an event, the number of distributors they signed up, and the number of sales (or dollar amount) for the week.

Another recommended KPI is "3-way calls". Distributors report the number of calls they made to their upline "expert," to get their prospect's questions answered and to allow their upline (or another distributor) to close those prospects. They also report the number of 3-way calls they received from distributors on their team. (See *Recruit and Grow Rich* for details on how to make and receive 3-way calls.)

Each distributor reports their numbers for the previous week and their goal for the coming week. As their teams grow, you may also have them report the numbers for their team (who aren't on the call).

For example, they may report that they personally had 2 guests at the local business overview and their team had a total of 7 guests.

As the facilitator of the call, you record their numbers and use them as a benchmark for working with them after the call.

If you someone's numbers are going up, you would praise them and help them set a bigger goal. If their numbers are going down, (e.g., less activity and/or fewer results), you would offer to work with them to help them adjust their goals and/or their activity.

You may report your own numbers on the call, or report your numbers on an accountability call conducted by your upline.

Accountability calls force distributors to publicly reveal their activity or lack thereof. This motivates them to consistently set and meet weekly benchmarks that are consistent with achieving their goals. It also creates a bit of competition among participants on the call, inspiring them to continually improve their effort and their results.

Accountability is a powerful motivator. When you know that you will be reporting what you do each week, you are compelled to do it. It keeps you from slacking off.

On the other hand, you will find under-performing distributors dropping off the call. This is normal. They may be embarrassed reporting zeros every week while listening to the successes of other distributors. The ones who stick with it, however, typically increase their performance and take their business to a much higher level.

Sometimes, distributors miss a call. You can have them report their numbers on the next call, but remind them that it is important to be on every call, for the sake of the others on the call and to keep themselves accountable.

If they continually miss calls, you should ask them to leave the call and perhaps come back when they're ready to be consistent. Otherwise, you'll be promoting poor work habits and inconsistent activity, which will create a downward spiral and hurt your team's production.

Some people say accountability in general, and accountability calls or groups in particular, can be counterproductive. They say they put too much pressure on distributors to perform, perhaps before they're ready. If they can't handle that pressure, they may not only drop off the call but out of the business.

The solution is to make sure your team sets goals that aren't too far out of reach, and frequently adjusting those numbers so that they can reach them more often than not. You want them to stretch, not break.

Teams that use accountability calls usually find an overall increase in growth. Some distributors drop out but the ones who stay often dramatically increase their numbers.

Workout partners

Workout partners are distributors who agree to help each other build their businesses. They make calls together, practice their scripts and approaches, sit together at trainings and compare notes, and hold each other accountable.

As with an accountability call, workout partners regularly report their numbers to each other. These reports are generally less detailed and structured, however.

Workout partners may do a 5-minute daily check-in, for example, to report the number of exposures and sign-ups they did that day, and the numbers they're aiming for the next day.

Unlike accountability calls, these calls aren't just about numbers. Workout partners may talk about the approaches they're using, role-play an upcoming follow-up call, or ask their partner for feedback or advice.

Workout partners are usually at or near the same level in the comp plan. They might compete with each other to see who gets to the next level first, but they also help each other to get there. They offer each other accountability and encouragement.

Some distributors might say they don't need or want a workout partner. You should encourage them to at least give it a try. Most distributors find it helpful to have someone to talk to who is going through the same things they are going through.

The best place for distributors to find a workout partner is at their local event. Introduce your distributors to each other, but it's fine if they choose a partner on another team.

By the way, make sure you have a workout partner yourself so you can share with your team how doing so has helped you.

Contests/promotions

You don't have to rely solely on what the company does in terms of contests. You can conduct your own.

You can offer prizes and awards for those who reach the next level in the compensation plan or beat their previous results. You can run promotions to get your team to reach higher: "Whoever gets three recruits this week. . ." or "The three top producing distributors this month. . ." or "Whoever has the most guests at the luncheon. . ."

You can also piggyback on company promotions, e.g., "Whoever qualifies for the bonus trip this month will be invited to a special dinner I'm hosting. . ."

You don't have to spend a lot of money on prizes. Get creative. You might offer to do a special training for the winning team (or get your upline to do it). If you run an event, you could provide front-row seating for a month or do on-stage recognition.

Tools make good prizes because if they use those tools, e.g., pass out DVDs or magazines to more prospects, or make calls to the leads you give them, they will be helping their business even more.

Books and training materials on network marketing and personal development also make excellent prizes.

Calling events

Encourage your team to get together for calling parties. Tell them to bring their phones and their lists. Have some bottled water and light snacks available. After the event, you can all go out to lunch or dinner together.

At the events, distributors learn how to get better at prospecting and inviting and answering questions by listening to how other distributors do it. Distributors also help each other by speaking with and closing each others prospects.

In addition, the buzz of five or ten distributors working the phones together creates an atmosphere where most distributors do more than they might do if they were alone. I've seen distributors do more exposures in one hour of group dialing than they usually do in a week.

You can get your team to do even more, and make the events more fun, by offering prizes to distributors who get the most exposures, the most sign-ups, or the most guests coming to the next event.

Build culture

Encourage your team to get together socially. No work, just fun. This helps them feel that they are part of something bigger, a team, not just a collection of individuals.

They'll make friends, deepen relationships, and possibly meet a future spouse.

Building culture can keep distributors around longer. Even if they're doing nothing today, or not getting the results they want, having friends in the business might keep them around longer, until they develop the confidence and skills to achieve their goals.

Building culture can also keep distributors from leaving and joining another company, simply because they don't want to leave their friends.

The one thing you should never do

As mentioned earlier, when I started in the business, I pushed my team. I pushed them to recruit, I pushed them to show up at the events, I pushed them to get on the team calls. I pushed so much I pushed some of them out of the business.

Don't make the mistake I made.

When you push most people, they back away. If you push too hard or too often, you risk alienating them and causing them to shut down or quit.

When you push a new distributor, they think, "I don't think this is the business for me." When you push an experienced distributor, they think, "Back off, I don't work for you."

Pushing your team is not good leadership.

If you are trying to qualify for a promotion or bonus and you push them too hard, they can "smell" your desperation. It looks like you're using them to build your business and that the only one you care about is yourself.

The best way to work with your team and get more production out of them is to zero in on what they want out of the business and then help them get it. As they reach their goals, you'll reach yours.

If you need 15 more team sales for the month to earn a promotion, for example, call through your team and find five distributors who need three personal sales to qualify for *their* next promotion. Work with them, help them get promoted, and you will get promoted.

As Zig Ziglar famously said, *"You can get everything you want in life if you will help enough other people get what they want."*

If you have a workout partner or a distributor on your team who has asked you to hold them accountable, a little pushing is okay. But there's a big difference between a little nudge and a big shove.

The best way to push a distributor is to remind them of what they said they were going to do and contrast that with what they actually did. Follow these three steps:

1. Remind them that they asked you to hold them accountable and verify that they still want you to do that,

2. Remind them of what they said they were going to do (their goals, activity level), and

3. Ask questions about their activity so they can see why they didn't reach their goals.

It's like holding up a mirror so they can see themselves.

Once they see that they're not doing what they need to do, ask them what they think they need to change. As always, offer to help them.

If you have lost some distributors because you pushed them too hard, you may be able to get them back with a simple apology. Tell them you're sorry for pushing so hard, you didn't realize what you were doing or you were up against a deadline and panicked. Tell them you have learned your lesson and you won't do it again.

Sometimes, that's all it takes to get a dormant distributor up and running again.

Multi-level marketing math

Bill is on your team and is close to earning a promotion this month. It comes with a nice bonus. You ask Bill if you can help him qualify but sadly, Bill has given up. There is less than a week left in the month and Bill doesn't think he can make it. It looks like he's not even going to try.

But you know he he could do it. There is enough time. You tell him not to give up.

You tell him that other distributors (you?) have been in his position and made it. You encourage him to go for it and offer to help.

Bill isn't sure. He says he's too busy. He'll do it next time. But you know that if he doesn't make it this month, there may not be a next time. If he doesn't make it, Bill might get discouraged and drop out of the business.

You also know that if he *does* make it this month, there's a good chance he will get excited and start building for the next promotion.

You're not ready to give up on him. You remind him that he doesn't have to do everything himself, that the business is called "multi-level" marketing for a reason.

"Bill, do you think that if you and I work together we could recruit just one person on your list?"

Bill agrees that this might be possible but points out that it won't be enough to get the promotion.

"Well, what if you and I also work with your new distributor and help them recruit just one person. That should be even easier because they will be brand new and have a fresh list of prospects."

Bill agrees with this, too but still doesn't see how this would be enough for him to get the promotion.

You continue, "So now you have two new distributors on your team. But we're not done. There's enough time for us to work with your new partners and help them each recruit one or two new distributors, maybe more. And you'll get credit for the sales that come with those new distributors."

Bill is adding up the numbers in his head. He's starting to see the light. He's starting to see that he doesn't have to do everything on his own.

"Don't forget, prospects who don't sign up in the business often buy product and we can also count those sales towards your promotion. When you add everything up, you could easily have enough volume to put you over the top."

Bill is getting excited. He sees that qualifying really is possible. With your help, he's ready to go for it.

You've helped Bill to understand the power of network marketing to quickly build a business. Before, he only thought about what he could do by himself. He was thinking like a sales person, not a business owner. Now he sees that his success doesn't depend solely on his own effort. He understands that by recruiting even one new distributor and helping them to do the same, he could quickly scale up his business.

Many distributors understand this. It's probably why they signed up in the first place. But like Bill, sometimes distributors need to be reminded that network marketing and sales are very different.

In network marketing you don't have to do everything yourself. You find some people and help them find some people and your organization grows, not by addition but by multiplication.

Your efforts compound. One distributor becomes two. Two becomes four. Four becomes eight. Soon, you have a very large organization.

Any time you work with someone who is discouraged about having a small team, or no team, show them the power of compounding. Show them that if they sign up a few new people who are ready to go to work, through compounding, their small organization can become a large organization.

"But I've already talked to everyone. . ."

Distributors often give up because they think they've talked to everyone they know. They say, "I've gone through my list," "I don"t know anyone else to talk to," or "Nobody's interested".

Sound familiar?

Many people quit because they think they don't have anyone else to approach. But they're wrong. They haven't talked to "everyone". They've probably contacted only a fraction of the people they know.

If you've ever asked a new distributor to show you their list and there are only ten or twenty names on it, you know what I'm telling you is true.

Experts tell us the average person knows *hundreds* of people. So when a distributor tells you that they've they've "talked to everyone," before you even think about talking to them about buying leads or prospecting in the cold market, help them to see that they know many more people than they realize.

You can

— Sit with them while they go through the contact list in the mobile phone and help them to see all of the names they passed over. You can also give them a "memory jogger" to help them remember people they know whose names might not be in their phone.

— Remind them about what they learned in training about not prejudging anyone. Tell them stories about other distributors who thought their neighbor or brother-in-law wouldn't be interested, only to see them walking across stage at the next convention.

— Explain that it doesn't matter if someone isn't interested, they can still buy product, and they can still give you referrals.

— Explain that someone might not be interested today but things could change in a few months. Contact them now and "take them off the market," so that when their situation has changed and they're ready to take another look at the business, they talk to you and nobody else.

— Explain that they don't have to approach everyone on their list but they should write down everyone's name, "because it will help you to recall the names of other people you know".

(Example: they might not want to approach their family doctor but by writing down the doctor's name, they might recall the name of someone who uses the same doctor they hadn't put on their list).

Sit them down and show them how to greatly expand their list. Let them see that they have many more contacts than they realize. Your goal is to add enough names so that they can recruit at least one distributor.

When I'm working with a new distributor, I sit with them or stay on the phone with them until they have at least 30 names. That is usually enough to recruit one or two distributors.

I also tell them to keep going until they have at least 100 names. That almost always guarantees they will recruit some distributors and make some sales.

Once they recruit someone, they'll realize that the business works and they'll want to keep going.

If they won't add more names to their list, or they add some but not enough, don't argue with them. Remember, you can't force anyone to do the business.

There's a reason they don't want to add any names to their list. This goes back to what we talked about earlier. They are afraid of rejection, and that's because they don't yet fully believe in the business or in themselves.

What can you do about that?

Re-recruit them. Start over, as if they are a new prospect.

Find out what they want and show them how your business can help them get it. If you know their "why," re-visit it with them. "I thought you told me you were doing this so you could spend more time with your kids. You still want to do that, don't you?"

Go over the comp plan again and show them what's possible.

If they love the product(s), share more success stories about how the products have helped people.

Introduce them to other distributors who will share their stories, especially stories about how they overcame their doubts and fears (and a small list) and went on to great success.

Get them to the events where they can get caught up in the energy and excitement and hear even more stories.

If none of this works, if they can't get past their fears and at least make an effort, let them go. Just like you would let go of a prospect who isn't ready to sign up.

Remember, your job isn't to convince anyone.

Let them go, but stay in touch with them because things may change and you want to be there when they're ready to push their fears aside and get the business going.

What if they really have talked to everyone?

If they really have gone through their warm market list, it's time to talk to them about the cold market.

Let them know that the cold market is harder and that going through their warm market first prepares them for it. Also, going through their warm market first will help them do a better job of helping their team go through their warm market.

Your distributor may have a small list or a list of people who aren't interested, but some of the people they recruit will have big lists and lots of interested people. Your distributor will be much better at helping their new recruit build their team as result of learning how to approach their warm market.

Also let them know that while the cold market is harder than the warm market, it has a few advantages.

First, the cold market is virtually unlimited. You will never run out of prospects.

Second, you can target the types of prospects you want to target. You can buy business opportunity or network marketing leads, you can cold call or network with business owners or professionals, and otherwise target the kinds of prospects you want to recruit.

Third, because you don't know the people you contact in the cold market, you don't have to be nervous about making a good impression or worry about them finding out that you're just getting started. In their eyes, you are who you say you are.

This also means that if you mess up, you can hang up the phone and talk to someone else. Unlike the warm market, you won't ever talk to those people again if you don't want to.

Explain the various cold market options that are available so they can choose what they want to do. They will probably ask what you're doing, and want to do that, but if they're not ready for it, you need to tell them that.

You might be good at cold calling professionals, for example, but that doesn't mean they should start with that. Tell them how you got started in the cold market and suggest that they start there, too.

How to motivate unmotivated distributors

Let's say you have a distributor on your team who is isn't motivated. She's not doing what you know she could do or she's not doing anything at all.

You've tried encouraging her. You've talked to her about her why. You've talked to her about all of the money she could be earning. You've offered to help.

But nothing happens.

Sound familiar? Sure. We all have lots of distributors like this on our team. Lots of zeros. Lots of people who aren't motivated to do more.

If your distributor isn't motivated to build her business, there's nothing you can do to change their mind.

There is something you can do, however, that might make her *want* to change her mind.

Let's say your unmotivated distributor is named Liz. She knows that by recruiting some new people she could increase her income. She likes the idea of that but her "desire for gain" isn't strong enough to get her to go to work.

Instead of appealing to her desire for gain, you can do something far more powerful. You can invoke her "fear of loss".

Science has proven that humans are more likely to take action to protect something they already own than they are to acquire something of similar value. If I promise to give you two crisp one-hundred dollar bills if you call an extra 20 prospects tonight, for example, you may or may not do it.

An extra two hundred dollars (on top of the money you might earn from signing up some of those prospects) would be nice to have but are you willing to make an extra 20 calls tonight to get it?

Maybe. Maybe not.

On the other hand, if you lost your wallet with two hundred dollars in it, I'm betting you would look everywhere for it—house, car, under dressers, in the seat cushions—and you would continue looking until you find it.

Your fear of losing two hundred dollars would motivate you, whereas your desire for gaining two hundred dollars might not.

Fear of loss is a powerful motivator and you can use it to get your team to do what they might otherwise won't do.

Let's say Liz is front-line to you. If she has any distributors under her, the first thing you should do is take inventory of them and find at least one distributor who wants to build their business. Work with that distributor and help them recruit and make some sales.

As the distributor under Liz recruits and builds his or her team, contact Liz and share with her how well this distributor is doing. Say nice things about them. Make a fuss about their growing business.

Also tell Liz about the new people that are now on her team. Tell her how excited they are to get to work and how excited you are to help them and watch their teams grow.

As this group starts adding new distributors and making more sales, stay in touch with Liz. Don't ask her to do anything; you already tried that. Just keep her informed about what's going on "under" her.

As the team under Liz continues to grow, continue to inform her and share your excitement.

Then, when you think the time is right, tell Liz about how much money she is missing out on because she's not qualified to get overrides from that leg.

Remind her that the distributor under her is now at the same level she is and that for Liz to get overrides she needs to get promoted (or whatever the reason she's not qualified to get overrides).

Do the math for her. Estimate how much she's losing. Let her see that she's losing $1500 a month (or whatever) in overrides that **pass by her and are paid to you** as her upline. Thank her for leading you to this distributor.

At this point, don't be surprised to hear her ask you what she needs to do to get that promotion and earn those overrides. If she doesn't, contact her again the following month and tell her how much she's now losing. Continue reporting to her how much she's losing until she can't stand it anymore!

Trust me, fear of loss is a powerful tool. I know, because my upline used it with me when I wasn't doing what he knew I was capable of doing.

Early in my career, after I worked my way up to a top position in our comp plan, I had fallen off for a couple of months. As a result of not being qualified, around $4,000 per month in overrides was being paid to my upline instead of me.

My upline thanked me for of the extra money. He reminded me that if I re-qualified, I would get these overrides instead of him.

Boy, did that light a fire under me!

I could think of nothing else than getting re-qualified. I worked day and night to do it and once I did, I never failed to qualify again.

My upline might have told me how I could have increased my income by $4,000 per month. That might or might not have motivated me. But LOSING $4,000 a month? Money that was supposed to come to me but wasn't? My money, flowing right by me and into the hands of someone else?

Painful. And motivating. Like nothing else I've ever seen.

So that's the strategy. Find someone down-line from your "Liz" and help them grow. Point to them and tell your Liz how much she's losing because she's not qualified for those overrides.

Now, let's say that Liz has a distributor many levels deep in her organization named Kristie. You start working with Kristie and help her recruit and grow her business.

Before you contact Liz, however, you talk to Kristie's sponsor, Lauren, who is obviously also under Liz. You tell Lauren how great Kristie is doing. You say things like, "She's going all the way in this business!" You tell Lauren the level Kristie is shooting for, or the money she is on track to earn (or whatever else you think might get Lauren's attention).

And then you ask Lauren if she wants to do the same.

Point out that if she gets to work like Kristie, she can override Kristie and her team.

Next, you talk to Lauren's sponsor. Tell her what's going on in her organization and ask her if she wants to get going. Tell her what she would have to do and offer to help her do it.

Keep doing this up the line, until you reach Liz and tell her about all of the activity going on in her organization.

This is called "burning from the bottom up". You use "fear of loss" to help start a fire deep in a leg. That fire burns upwards, motivating some or all of the distributors in that line or leg, all the way to the top.

Now, Liz has an even bigger decision to make. She has a leg that's "on fire". If she doesn't do something, over time, she is going to lose big time. That fear of loss will often be all it takes to get her (and others in that leg) to get to work to protect what is theirs.

This strategy can help you take a leg that is "doing nothing" and turn it into a powerful, thriving, profitable profit center for you.

What if there's nobody to work with in that leg?

Let's say Liz doesn't have any distributors under her who are willing to get to work. Or any distributors under her at all. What then?

You might consider "placing" some of *your* new recruits under her.

You put your new recruit, Joe, under Liz, and work with him.

Then you put your next recruit under Joe. You continue putting new recruits under each other, in one leg under Liz, until you find someone who gets busy on their own.

I've seen some distributors place new recruits twenty deep in a leg before finding a leader. Sometimes, the leader is someone they placed in that line. Sometimes it's someone recruited by a distributor in that line. But eventually, the leader shows up and brings the leg to life.

Why put them only under one leg? Because if you build more legs under Liz and "force" her to get promoted, you'll cut yourself off from overrides that will go to her. The goal of placing under Liz isn't to build her business for her, it is to create a fear of loss in her so she will go build her other legs.

Distributors who are against "placing" say it breeds weakness and can cost the upline (you) a fortune in lost overrides once "Liz" gets promoted. These distributors instead put most or all of their recruits front line to them.

Proponents of placing point out that if you only build one leg for a distributor, there is very little risk. If they don't do anything, they won't get promoted (or they will only get promoted a level or two, depending on your comp plan). If they build more legs and get promoted, you will earn more overrides from those new legs than you might lose from the first leg you built.

More ways to use placing

You can also use placing as a tool to inspire your team to recruit more than they are already recruiting. For example, you might tell your team, "I've got a new guy signing up on Friday. I'll put him under the first distributor who signs up a new distributor this week."

If you have a distributor who is working the business and getting results, but perhaps not enough results because they haven't yet hit their stride or because they're working two or three jobs, putting some distributors under them might inspire them to put more time or energy into the business.

I've seen this work.

A top-recruiter and top money-earner in our company was not a good recruiter when she started in the business. Her upline saw potential in her and put some of his new recruits under her. Eventually, she grew into the powerhouse she is today.

You can also use "placing" to get prospects who are on the fence to make a decision.

You might tell them, "I've got a new guy signing up on Friday. He's got a lot of experience in network marketing and has a big list. If you sign up *today*, I'll put him under you."

When the new guy signs up on Friday, you then have *two* new recruits to place. You can then go to a third prospect and tell them you have signed up two new distributors; if he (the third prospect) signs up, you'll put both new distributors under them.

I've seen distributors recruit a lot of people this way.

Placing may or may not be right for you. Talk to your upline and to other distributors in your company and see what they do and recommend.

Ultimately, your decision to do it may come down to how many distributors you recruit each month.

If you recruit only one or two distributors, placing is probably not a good strategy for you. Put your recruits front line. If they go to work, you'll be closer to the money; there won't be anyone between you, taking some of your overrides.

If you recruit ten or fifteen distributors each month, on the other hand, placing some of them may be a viable tool for you.

Also, you may not have time to work with all of your new recruits. Putting some of them under others on your team who don't recruit as many but have the skills (and time) to work with these new recruits could benefit everyone.

Someone once said there are three types of distributors in network marketing. The first are self-motivated. They don't need much in the way of help from you. You don't need to place anyone under them.

The second type are "motivatable". They aren't self-motivated but can be motivated to get to work. Placing some recruits under them might invoke a fear of loss and get them to do that.

The third type of distributor is "unmotivatable". They aren't going to do anything in the business, no matter what.

The problem is you can't always tell who is and who isn't motivatable. Placing is one way to find out.

Finding leaders

You want leaders on your team. They are the ones who build big organizations and make a lot of money for themselves, and for you.

Sometimes, they just show up. You recruit them or someone in your organization recruits them and off they go. They start recruiting and their team starts growing.

If you or someone on your team has the good fortune to recruit a leader, great. Support them, help them when they ask for it, but mostly, get out of their way and enjoy the overrides.

Unless they come from a network marketing background, however, most network marketing leaders don't start out fully formed. It takes some time for them to learn the network marketing business model and develop their skills.

I know. I was one of them.

Although I had built a successful law practice and other (regular) businesses, I was new to network marketing and network marketing is different from other businesses. It takes a different set of skills and a different mindset.

I did it by paying attention to the leaders in my upline and elsewhere in the company. I watched and listened to the way they spoke to prospects, how they did a presentation, how they did a training, and how they worked with their team. I got into their circle-ups and listened in on their leadership calls. I soaked up every ounce of information I could and used it to build my team.

I also recruited and worked with a lot of people. I made a lot of mistakes and learned from them. And from all of that, I eventually grew into a network marketing leader.

Identifying potential leaders

In *Recruit and Grow Rich*, I said that you don't need to become a leader to be successful in network marketing. If you recruit enough people, you will find leaders, even if you don't become one yourself.

I also said that it is better to become a leader because you will grow faster, attract more leaders, and build a bigger business than you otherwise might if you don't become a leader yourself.

Either way, you'll want to be able to identify potential leaders in your organization so you can support them and help them grow.

How do you do that? How do you identify potential leaders?

Earlier, we talked about the process of taking inventory. You systematically call through your genealogy list and ask everyone if they are ready to get to work or increase their activity and get to the next level.

Some distributors will tell you that they are ready but they really aren' t. Since you can't work with everyone, as your team grows, you'll need a better way to identify who is truly ready and worthy of your time and attention.

Here are some ways to do that.

What are your numbers this month?

You can look at your genealogy and see who is recruiting and producing in your organization but, as Ron pointed out to me, this might not tell you the whole story. You may have distributors who aren't yet getting significant results (or any results) but have a lot of activity that will soon bring results.

One way to identify these potential leaders is to take inventory by asking about their results and their activity.

You can ask questions like:

— How close are you to [qualifying, hitting a goal]? What do you need to get done?
— How many distributors are you looking to recruit this month?
— How many sales are you shooting for this month? How close are you to that number?
— How many prospects do you have in your pipeline right now?
— How many daily exposures are you doing?
— How many guests do you have coming to next week's event?
-- How do your numbers look this month compared to last month?

You want to know their personal numbers *and* their team's numbers.

A leader will know how many recruits his team is doing (and who is recruiting them). They'll know their team's production for the previous month and how the current month looks in comparison.

Ask them to identify who is working on their team so you can reach out to them yourself. Find out who is close to qualifying/getting promoted, etc., or who is working hard to get there. Keep track of the "workers" on their team; they might be your next leader.

What if their numbers aren't good? What if nothing is happening for them personally or on their team?

That's okay. Their actual numbers aren't as important as their attitude.

They may have little or nothing going on, or be far away from hitting their target, but if they are positive and optimistic, if they say they want things to change and they are open to your help, that's good. Help them.

A new game plan, spending some time with you and watching you make calls, additional training, or simply telling them that you believe in them and know they can make it, can go a long way towards getting someone to move forward.

If not much is happening and they don't seem to care, that's a different story.

Don't pend a lot of time with someone like that. You can't help people who don't want to be helped. Move on.

Remember, you're taking inventory to find potential leaders. Someone you can work with. Anyone who doesn't care doesn't qualify.

Finally, if they don't know their numbers, let them know why it is important that they do. Encourage them to look and let you know. If they don't get back to you, you'll know that they aren't a potential leader or worthy of your time. At least not yet.

Did you know. . . Do you want to go for it?

Another approach is to call and share some news that could

benefit your distributors if they take action, followed by asking them if they plan to take that action. For example:

— Did you know you're only 3 points away from the Mega-distributor level this month? You're going for it, aren't you?

— Did you know that Bob Bigshot is in town and he's speaking here on Tuesday night. How many guests are you shooting for?

— Did you hear about the bonus trip they just announced? You're going to qualify, right? (Or, "How many people on your team do you plan to have with you on the trip?")

— Did you hear that Mary just earned her pin? Will you get yours this month or next month?

You want them to get excited and say yes, they want to go for "it". If they don't, you can explore this with them or you can move on. If they want to go for it, ask them what you can do to help.

Will I See You There?

Another way to take inventory is to call and invite everyone to the next event, whether that is put on by your team, the company or by you. Keep track of who says they're coming and who shows up.

If they tell you they're not coming (because they don't see the value in the event), you need to have a talk with them and possibly get them on the phone with your upline to help them understand why they need to be there.

Someone who consistently says they're not coming, or makes excuses for why they didn't show up, is not someone who deserves your personal time.

I'm forming a "core team"

One of the best ways to find potential leaders and help them develop into a leader is to form a core team. This is a handful of key people in your organization who are serious about building their business.

You'll meet with your core team on a weekly conference call where you (and/or guest speakers) will provide additional training, exchange ideas, and share stories, tips and encouragement.

You might have everyone discuss the "book of the week" you're all reading or take turns summarizing a different chapter.

Your core team shares their successes, their challenges, their questions, and their advice about what has been working for them.

A core team allows you to stay close to your leaders and potential leaders so you can help them grow.

Now, once you have started your core team, you can use it to take inventory.

When I started my first core team, I contacted distributors who were producing and/or doing the activities (e.g., showing up at the events, doing 3-way calls, etc.).

I said:

"I'm putting together a "core team" and I'm looking for a few key people who are serious about the business and are ready to take things to a higher level".

Note that I used the term "key people" to let them know that not everyone would be invited or accepted. Who doesn't want to be thought of as a key person?

I explained that my core team would receive extra attention from me, including priority on taking their calls and more of my time helping them build the business. I would make calls with them if they wanted, I would help them train their new distributors, and I would teach them the things that I had learned or was learning from my mentors in the business.

I told them that the core team was about developing leaders. I expected them to do what leaders do: be on the team call every week, come to all the local events, do daily exposures, and so on.

They would also be expected to get on my core team conference call each week. There would be training from me and from guest speakers in our upline and other successful distributors in the company.

I let them know that there would be other things expected of them in terms of activity and performance. I didn't go into specifics on that first call, however. I simply wanted to know if they were interested and willing to commit.

Some distributors said they weren't interested. (They usually said something like, "I don't think I have time for that," or "I'm not ready for that yet." That was fine. They were being honest and I respect that. Not everyone is a leader or ready to become one.

I found this an excellent way to take inventory and identify distributors who at least said they were ready to become a leader.

Over time, many distributors fell off the core team and others were added. Many leaders formed their own core teams and duplicated the process, stepping up into their role as leaders.

Your core team might start out with just you and one other distributor. That's fine. Your numbers will grow. For now, it is an excellent way to take inventory and identify potential leaders.

Forming a core team has another benefit. When the rest of your team learns about it and that it is by invitation only, many distributors will work harder to get that invitation. They'll want to be included in your inner circle and not be left behind.

Show me your calendar

Another way to evaluate whether someone is worthy of your time is to wait until they contact you, seeking your help or advice. At that point, you can talk to them about their results and their activity, to see if they are really working.

I have a friend in the business who makes his distributors provide proof of their activity. If you call and ask for his help and he suspects that you aren't doing the activities, the first thing he does is ask you to send him a copy of your calendar.

He also has a form you can fill out and send him so he can see your numbers.

He wants to see how many appointments you had the previous week, and how many team calls or training calls or recruiting calls you were on. He wants to know how many exposures or sit-downs you did, how many prospects you put on a 3-way call, and how many guests you invited to the weekly event.

He wants to know your numbers because he knows that the numbers tell the story.

You may not be getting a lot of results (which is probably the reason you contacted him) but he knows that if you're doing the activity, the results will come. He wants his team to see that for themselves.

If a distributor isn't doing the activities, there's little he can do to help them other than to tell tell them that this is why they're not getting results.

If they are doing the activities and still not getting results, he'll talk to them, help them figure out the problem, and advise them on how to improve.

In other words, if you're on his team and you want his help, you have to prove to him that you're worth it.

You can use this with your team. Ask them to show you their numbers (or their calendar) so you know whether or not they're working.

Bringing dead distributors back to life

I've got good news and bad news for you. The bad news is something you've probably figured out: people quit.

Lots of them and for different reasons.

You never know who it will be or when it might happen. No matter what you do or how hard you work, every month people quit your business.

Even leaders quit. Big money-earners quit. People you've gotten close to and thought would be with you forever quit.

Sometimes they quit by officially dropping their distributor status with the company. Usually, they just drift away.

It's called *attrition* and it's a natural part of network marketing. You may be able to slow it down but you'll never stop it completely.

So that's the bad news. The good news is that attrition doesn't have to stop you. You can still build a hugely successful business.

How? By staying ahead of the it.

If you and your team bring in more distributors each month than drop out, your business will continue to grow.

If your team loses 10 distributors this month but you're bringing in 40 or 50 or 100 new distributors, attrition won't hurt you. You'll stay ahead of it. The new recruits will replace the ones who leave and your numbers will be bigger each month than the month before.

Does that mean you can never slow down or retire? Not at all. It means you have to build your team with multiple leaders in multiple legs so that when you want to slow down or retire, your leaders will take over. They'll continue to build (until they're ready to retire), and train their teams to do the same.

In the corporate world, employees come and go. People quit or are fired and new ones are hired to take their place. As the company grows, new employees are hired. The company survives and grows no matter who is at the top. Your business will, too.

Don't give up on anyone

So distributors quit, never to be heard from before. They'll tell themselves they "tried" network marketing and it didn't work for them. They say they are done being an entrepreneur and go back to whatever they were doing before, or they will look for another network marketing opportunity.

They're done. So long, farewell, have a good life.

But not everyone is like that. Some will come back. It happens more often than you think.

I've seen more than a few distributors leave our company, try one or two other companies, and then come back to ours and finally get to work. Once they realize that the grass isn't greener on the other side, or they are in a different place in their life, they sign up again.

Someone who signed up as a distributor did so because they wanted something. The odds are they still want the same thing. That's why you see distributors repeatedly signing up with different companies, continuing to look for what they're missing.

For this reason, many network marketers focus their recruiting efforts on prospects who have been in network marketing before. The theory is, "If they signed up once, they'll sign up again."

Well guess what? Sometimes they sign up with the same company.

I did that. A long time ago I signed up with a company and dropped out in less than a year. I liked what the company was doing, but I wasn't ready to commit to the business. I was busy building my law practice so, as they say, "the timing wasn't right."

Years later, I was at a different place in my life and signed up again with the same company. The company I am with today. The company that gave me the opportunity to earn a six-figure passive income.

That opportunity was there the first time I signed up. I just wasn't ready for it.

Timing is everything.

That's true for distributors who don't drop out. The ones on our teams who are doing nothing.

I've seen distributors sign up and do nothing, wake up years later and finally get to work.

I'll see in my stats that someone who has never done anything, or hasn't done anything in a long time, suddenly make a sale or recruit a distributor. Or I'll get a call or email from someone I haven't heard from in years (or who I have never talked to), telling me they're finally ready to "get this thing going".

I'm sure it's the same in your company.

What does this tell us? It tells us that dead distributors come back to life. That's why you must regularly take inventory of your team, and don't leave out the ones who are doing nothing.

Some of them are ready to work. They're there. I promise you. Keep calling and you'll find them.

But don't stop there. Go through your genealogy and find distributors who have officially "dropped" from the business.

Call and recruit them again.

Ask them why they never got going or why they dropped. Maybe they weren't ready before and maybe they are now. Maybe their sponsor didn't help them and they felt abandoned. Maybe they didn't know about the good things happening in the company.

Hearing from you might make all the difference.

There are many reasons why people stop working or quit. Illness, marital issues, loss of a job, kids in trouble, a death in the family. It's a long list. But things change. Kids go off to college, a baby is born and the mother wants to be able to work from home, a spouse retires and has more time or needs more income, and all of sudden, they're ready.

Make sure you stay in touch with your dormant and dropped

distributors. Email them with news about the company, products, or your team. Let them know how some other distributors they may remember are doing. Let them know about your progress.

But gently. Never push. A friend staying in touch with a friend.

Keep your name in front of them and remind them that you're still in the business. If and when they're ready to get to work (or sign up again), you want them to know that you're ready to help.

You may not hear back from them for months or even years. Don't give up on them. Stay in touch. When they're ready, they'll let you know.

Network marketing experts often say, "It's easier to give birth than to resurrect the dead," meaning it is easier to recruit new distributors than to get distributors who aren't doing anything to get going. That's often true. But sometimes, if the timing is right, it's easier to bring back to life someone who has been in the business before, or is still in the business but has gone to sleep.

And it happens often enough that you should get excited about the potential that lies hidden in your genealogy.

When I dropped out of the business years ago, my sponsor probably didn't notice. I don't even remember who my sponsor was. They didn't stay in touch with me or try to re-recruit me.

When I signed up again, it was with a different sponsor. I'm sure she's glad that my original sponsor didn't stay in touch with me because I've made my new sponsor a fortune.

How to dramatically increase your odds of success

When you get started in network marketing you start from zero. No customers, no team, no interested prospects. Just you and your hopes and dreams and plans to make something happen.

You're excited, but scared. You want to succeed, but you have doubts. You know you need to get things going, but you're not sure what to do.

Its not much different when you're getting re-started.

In order to get your business going, you have to create momentum. You need to overcome inertia and get some results.

If you can get those first few recruits and sales quickly, your odds of success go way up.

You'll have a team to work with and some cash in the bank. Your early results will motivate you to keep going.

You'll know the business works. You'll know you can recruit and make money.

You'll be excited and have energy. Your prospects will hear the excitement in your voice and be curious about what you're doing.

You won't care so much when prospects say no. You'll keep moving because you know there are people out there who will say yes.

Your early success will lead to more success. You'll be more confident. You'll get more results and they'll start coming more quickly. Your business will grow bigger and faster.

Because you have momentum.

Creating momentum in your business is like pushing a car that has run out of gas. The car is heavy. It takes a lot of effort to get it to move even a few inches. But then it gets easier. The force of the car's weight helps carry it forward.

That's how network marketing works. It takes a lot of effort at first, as you try to create momentum. Eventually, it gets easier. Your business is moving and you can keep it moving with a lot less effort.

Many new distributors (most?) have a difficult time creating momentum in their business because they start slowly. They're scared, they don't want to make mistakes or get rejected, so they hold back. They don't do enough activity to get some positive results.

Building slowly is painful. Everything is harder. Every "no" carries more weight. You have too much time to think about what you're doing and doubt yourself.

You may eventually achieve momentum by moving slowly but it takes a lot more time.

Building quickly is much easier.

When I was getting started, I was told about the value of creating momentum. My upline advised me to put everything else in my life aside for the first 90 days and focus on the business.

"Do as much as you can, as quickly as you can," he said. "That's how you create momentum."

And that's what I did.

I contacted everyone on my list as quickly as possible. I didn't study names and try to figure out the perfect approach for each prospect, I sped through the list and called everyone. I told them what I was doing and asked them to look at some information.

If they weren't interested in looking, I moved on. If they looked and weren't interested in the business, I move on. But because I moved quickly and talked to so many people, I quickly found some people who *were* interested and signed them up.

I signed up a bunch of distributors my first month that way. More the next month.

I didn't stop to learn the business, I learned as I went along. Within a few months, I was earning several thousand dollars a month. I kept running and went on to become a top recruiter in our company.

Because of that 90 day run, I had personal momentum.

I pushed my team too hard and made other mistakes, but I fixed that. Eventually, my team also achieved momentum and in a few years, I was earning a six-figure passive income.

If you want to get your business started or re-started and create momentum and dramatically increase your odds of success, don't start slowly, don't tiptoe, *run.*

Take massive action. Do it immediately. Don't slow down to think about what you're doing, just do it.

You may be looking at a lot of zeros in your organization right now. You know what? It doesn't matter. You can start over, right now, and become a new distributor again. The past is over. Forget it. Make today the first day of your new business.

And think big.

Grant Cardone, author of *The 10X Rule*, recommends setting goals that are 10X more than you think you want and then taking 10X the action you think is required to get there.

Big goals. Massive action.

It's not too late for you. Not at all. It's never too late. It doesn't matter where you are right now, you can get where you want to go.

And you can do it faster than you ever thought possible.

Brian Tracy, author of, *Create Your Own Future: How to Master the 12 Critical Factors of Unlimited Success*, talks about "The Principle of Accelerating Acceleration". He sees it, I believe, as a corollary of the "Law of Attraction," because he says "Whatever you are moving toward [i.e., a goal] begins moving toward you as well."

He goes on to say something I think every network marketer needs to hear:

"When you first set a new, big goal and begin moving toward it, your progress will often be quite slow. You may be frustrated

and think of giving up. The bigger your goal, the further away it will seem. You may have to work on it for a long time before you see any progress at all. But this is all part of the process of goal attainment.

The '20/80 rule' helps to explain the principle. . . . For the first 80 percent of the time that you are working toward your goal, you will only cover about 20 percent of the distance. However, if you persist and refuse to give up, you will accomplish the final 80 percent of your goal in the last 20 percent of the time that you spend working on it."

This means you're closer to reaching your goal than you think. Tracy continues:

*"Many people work for weeks, months, and even years toward a big goal and see little progress. They often lose heart and give up. But **what they didn't realize is that they had laid all of the groundwork necessary and were almost at the take-off point**. They were just about to start accelerating toward their goal, and their goal was about to start moving at a great speed toward them.*

*This principle of accelerating acceleration seems to apply to almost every big goal that you set for yourself. **You must therefore decide in advance that you will never give up**."* [emphasis mine]

In other words, even though you may see little or no progress in your business, if you keep going, things will change. You're closer to success than you know.

And, as Napoleon Hill put it in *Think and Grow Rich*, "When riches begin to come, they come so quickly, and in such abundance, that you will wonder where they have hiding during all those lean years."

Remember, it only takes a few

Your team may be doing little or nothing right now. You may have no team at all. But everything you have learned and done up to this point has not been wasted effort. You know a lot about what to do and a lot about what not to do. You have real-world experience. You've made mistakes, you've lived through the disappointments, and now you're ready to finally make things happen.

You can't sit back and wait for it to happen, however. You have to run, create momentum, and make it happen.

You may be the only one doing anything right now. In a few days, there could be two of you. The two of you will find more. In a few months, there could be dozens of you. In a few years, thousands.

To make this happen, you need to find a few people who share your desire to change their life.

A few. Not thousands. Not hundreds. Not even dozens. You need a few. Because those few will go out and find a few more. And through the power of compounding, the thousands will come.

Yes, it has to be the *right* few. You will have to recruit more than a few to find them. But find them you will.

How long will it take? That's not the right question. It will take as long as it takes.

Does it really matter if it takes you a few years longer than the next guy or gal? If you know you can achieve all of your goals in the business, a few years doesn't matter.

Recruit as many as you can, as quickly as you can, and have faith that everything will sort itself out.

Whatever you do, don't wait to get started. Start now.

For the next 90 days, put everything else aside and make your business a priority. Give it everything you've got, every ounce of energy and every minute of time.

After 90 days, assess your results. If you have done the work, you'll be amazed at how far you've come. And trust me, you'll be so excited, you'll want to do another 90-day run.

Start by taking inventory. Call everyone in your organization and find out who is ready to work. Tell them what you're doing and see if they want to join you.

You're looking for even one or two who are say they want to do it. Don't worry about the ones who don't.

Next, make a new warm market list. Buy some leads. And get to work.

It's not too late. You can fix your business. Go do it.

Relax and let it be easy

I came across a quote recently that I want to leave you with, by writer Alan Cohen. I hope it inspires you as it has inspired me. Cohen said, "How would I be doing this differently if I were willing to let it be easy?"

Too many people believe that success is difficult to achieve and, sure enough, for them it is. They think too much and act too little. They analyze everything, second guess everything, and complicate everything.

It doesn't have to be that way.

Yes, you have make the calls and do the work but it doesn't have to be painful or difficult. You talk to people on the phone about their hopes and dreams and show them how they can achieve them. Most say no, but if you talk to enough of them, some say yes. That's when it gets exciting.

You don't have to be good. Just busy.

Do yourself a favor. Pretend that you're the kind of person who finds the work easy. Let go of your resistance to change, lack of belief, and fear. Have faith in yourself. Believe in your goals. And get to work.

Let it be easy and it will be.

What's next?

Thank you for purchasing my book. If you found the information useful, please leave a review.

Even one sentence helps. Thank you!

And please tell others by sharing on FACEBOOK and TWITTER.

Remember, to get more recruiting tips and business building ideas, subscribe to my **FREE Recruiting Tips Newsletter**. You'll also be notified when I release new books or have a special offer.

To subscribe, go here:
http://recruitandgrowrichbook.com/newsletter

If you would like to send me your comments on this book, or suggestions for future books, please email me at recruitingbook@gmail.com

I'd love to hear from you.

—David M. Ward

About the author

David M. Ward is an attorney, business owner, marketing consultant, and author.

Ward started in network marketing to build retirement income and to escape the long hours of his law practice. "I was a victim of the self-employment trap--trading my time for dollars," he says. "The bigger my practice grew, the harder I had to work."

After twenty years, he was ready for a change. "Network marketing gave me the time freedom and financial freedom I always wanted."

Ward has been recognized as a six-figure income earner and top recruiter in his network marketing company. He and his wife live in southern California.

Other network marketing books by David M. Ward

Recruit and Grow Rich: How to Quickly Build a Successful Network Marketing Business by Recruiting Smarter, Not _Working Harder_

—_"The Best Network Marketing Book I've Ever Read!"_
—_"By Far The Best & Most Complete Resource for Network Marketing!"_
—_"Incredible Resource for Anyone in Network Marketing!"_

"Best MLM ebook of 2014 _. . .a must for any beginner or advanced network marketer. If I had to give my downline a book to learn network marketing with, this would be the book."_ —**Erik Christian**

Author David M. Ward is an attorney who started a network marketing business to build retirement income. His schedule only allowed him to work the business a few hours a week and his business grew slowly. Frustrated with his results, he set out to find ways to "recruit smarter" and quickly sign up more prospects.

His methods worked. In his first few years he signed up hundreds of distributors and created a six-figure passive income. In this book, Ward lays out the system he used to quickly identify interested prospects, expose them, and get them signed up--often in a single day.

http://recruitandgrowrich.com/kindle

* * *

Recruiting Up: How I Recruited Hundreds of Professionals in my Network Marketing Business, and How You Can, Too

"Recruiting up" means recruiting professionals, business owners, sales people, real estate agents, insurance brokers, financial planners, and other people with the talent and resources to build a successful network marketing business.

Author David M. Ward is an attorney who recruited hundreds of professionals in his network marketing business and built a six-figure passive income in just a few years. "When you recruit a lot of people who can recruit a lot of people," he says, "your business can grow very quickly."

In **Recruiting Up**, you'll learn how he did it, and how you can, too.

http://recruitingup.com

* * *

Network Marketing Made Simple: A Guide for Training New Distributors

". . .an invaluable tool for sponsors to provide their downline" — Donald Gravalec

"Helps prioritize activities that create income. A must read for any new distributor." — R. Pike

The best way to train a new distributor is to get them on the phone or out in the field talking to people. They need to recruit and make some money.

But first, they need to know the basics.

Network Marketing Made Simple teaches new distributors the basics of network marketing. It shows them how to get their business started, how to recruit and make money, and how to get to the next level.

You can use this book to train new distributors, as a teaching guide on team calls, or as a self-study guide. If you have a new distributor, or you are a new distributor, this is the book for you.

Network Marketing Made Simple
http://recruitandgrowrich.com/nmms

www.ingramcontent.com/pod-product-compliance
Lightning Source LLC
Chambersburg PA
CBHW070044210526
45170CB00012B/578